One Yelpy Kelpie

Jo Rothwell

Illustrated by Bryce Rothwell

1

One Yelpy Kelpie calling out Cooeee,

2

Two crazy
Kangas
catapulting
over
me.

3

Three spiky
Echidnas
licking
lots of
ants,

4

Four pretty Brolgas
waltzing
at the
dance.

5

Five stars
of the
Southern Cross
twinkling
in the
sky,

6

Six cheeky
Emus
gobbling
everything
they spy.

7

Seven single
thongs
searching
for
a pair,

8

Eight
dozing
Possums
snuggling
everywhere.

9

Nine crunchy
anzacs
served with
billy tea,

10

Ten digging
Wombats
tunnelling
under me.

11

Eleven cranky
Crocodiles
picking at
their teeth,

12

Twelve Crested
Cockatoos
fly and
squawk and
screech.

13

Thirteen
Tassie Devils
play and
scratch and
bite,

14

Fourteen busy
Bilbys
burrow
through the
night.

15

Fifteen buzzing
Blow Flies
landing on
their tea,

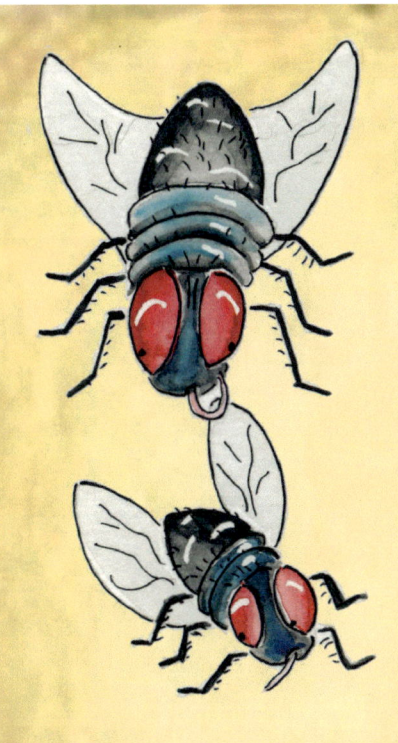

And those
fifteen
buzzing
Blow Flies
better keep
away
from
me!

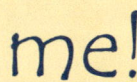

For BJ – Our very own Yelpy Kelpie
You gave us the most beautiful 18 years and
will be mustering butterflies in heaven.

Published by Rothwell Publishing,
Warburton, Victoria, Australia

www.rothwellpublsihing.com

First published 2013
Reprinted 2016, 2019, 2022, 2024
Text copyright (c) Jo Rothwell 2013
Illustrations copyright (C) Rothwell Publishing 2013

Printed in Australia

National Library of Australia Cataloguing-in-Publication entry

Rothwell, Jo, author

One Yelpy Kelpie / Jo Rothwell ; illustrated by Bryce Rothwell.

ISBN: 9780987391704 (paperback)
For pre school age
Animals--Counting--Juvenile Fiction.
Animals--Australia--Juvenile Fiction.

A823.4

Look out for further books and products by
Rothwell Publishing

www.rothwellpublishing.com

Made in the USA
Monee, IL
07 July 2026